modern

Southwest Afghans

Bold graphics in rich desert colors give these six afghans modern Southwest flair. Featuring medium or bulky weight yarn, the throws call for Easy to Intermediate crochet skills.

CONTENTS

LEISURE ARTS, INC. • Maumelle, Arkansas

AUTUMN

●●○○ EASY

Finished Measurement: 47½" x 56½" (120.5 cm x 143.5 cm)

SHOPPING LIST

Yarn (Medium Weight) 4 MEDIUM

[5 ounces, 251 yards
(142 grams, 230 meters) per skein]:

- ☐ Rust - 3 skeins
- ☐ Brown - 2 skeins
- ☐ Ecru - 2 skeins
- ☐ Green - 2 skeins

Crochet Hook

- ☐ Size J (6 mm)
  or size needed for gauge

GAUGE INFORMATION

One Strip = 6½" x 54" (16.5 cm x 137 cm)

Gauge Swatch: 2" wide x 9" long (5 cm x 22.75 cm)
With Green, ch 25.
Work same as Inner Strip Leaf Rnd, page 4: 2 Leaves.

STITCH GUIDE

TREBLE CROCHET ***(abbreviated tr)***

YO twice, insert hook in stitch indicated, YO and pull up a loop (4 loops on hook), (YO and draw through 2 loops on hook) 3 times.

INNER STRIP (Make 5)

With Green, ch 155.

Leaf Rnd (Right side)**:**

First Side - Slip st in second ch from hook and in next 2 chs, ★ † ch 2, dc in next ch, tr in next ch, 2 tr in each of next 2 chs, tr in next ch, dc in next ch, hdc in next ch †, sc in next ch, slip st in next 5 chs; repeat from ★ across to last 8 chs, then repeat from † to † once, (sc, slip st, sc) in last ch.

Second Side - Working in free loops of beginning ch ***(Fig. 2, page 22)***, ★ † hdc in next ch, dc in next ch, tr in next ch, 2 tr in each of next 2 chs, tr in next ch, dc in next ch, ch 2 **(Leaf made)** †, slip st in next 5 chs, sc in next ch; repeat from ★ across to ch at base of last hdc, then repeat from † to † once, slip st in next 3 chs; finish off: 12 Leaves.

Note: Loop a short piece of yarn around last dc made to mark Leaf Rnd as **right** side and to mark bottom edge.

Row 1:

First Side - With **right** side facing and working in Back Loops Only ***(Fig. 1, page 22)***, join Ecru with slip st in first slip st made on Leaf Rnd (at bottom edge); ch 4, tr in next 2 slip sts, ★ † skip next 2 chs, hdc in next dc, sc in next 6 tr, hdc in next dc, dc in next 2 sts †, tr in next slip st, working **around** next slip st ***(Fig. 4, page 23)***, tr in beginning ch, tr in next 3 slip sts; repeat from ★ 10 times **more**, then repeat from † to † once, ch 4, slip st in next slip st: 177 sts and 2 ch-4.

Second Side - Ch 4, working in Back Loops Only, ★ † dc in next 2 sts, hdc in next dc, sc in next 6 tr, hdc in next dc, skip next 2 chs †, tr in next 3 slip sts, working **around** next slip st, tr in beginning ch, tr in next slip st; repeat from ★ 10 times **more**, then repeat from † to † once, tr in next 2 slip sts, ch 4, slip st in last slip st; finish off: 177 sts and 2 ch-4.

Row 2:

First Side - With **right** side facing and working in both loops, join Brown with dc in top of ch-4 on First Side ***(see Joining With Dc page 22)***; dc in same st, skip next 2 sts, (2 dc, ch 1, 2 dc) in next st, ★ skip next 3 sts, (2 dc, ch 1, 2 dc) in next st; repeat from ★ across to last 2 dc, skip last 2 dc, 2 dc in top of ch-4; finish off: 44 ch-1 sps and 180 dc.

Second Side - With **right** side facing and working in both loops, join Brown with dc in top of ch-4 on Second Side; work same as First Side.

Row 3:

First Side - With **right** side facing, join Rust with dc in first dc on First Side; dc in same st, skip next dc, dc in sp **before** next dc ***(Fig. 3, page 22)***, ★ 3 dc in next ch-1 sp, skip next 2 dc, dc in sp **before** next dc; repeat from ★ across to last 2 dc, skip next dc, 2 dc in last dc; finish off: 181 dc.

Second Side - With **right** side facing, join Rust with dc in first dc on Second Side; work same as First Side.

Row 4:

First Side - With **right** side facing, join Rust with dc in first dc on First Side; ★ skip next dc, 3 dc in next dc, skip next dc, dc in next dc; repeat from ★ across; finish off.

Second Side - With **right** side facing, join Rust with dc in first dc on Second Side; work same as First Side.

Join Strips together as follows:

With **wrong** sides of marked ends together and working through inside loops **only** of long edges, join Rust with slip st in **last** dc; ch 1, working from **left** to **right**, ★ insert hook in st to right of hook ***(Fig. A)***, YO and draw through, under and to left of loop on hook (2 loops on hook) ***(Fig. B)***, YO and draw through both loops on hook ***(Fig. C)*** ***(reverse sc made, Fig. D)***; repeat from ★ across; finish off.

Fig. A

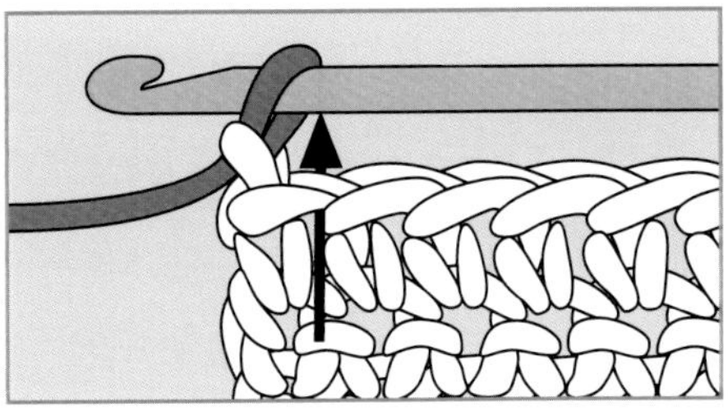

Fig. B

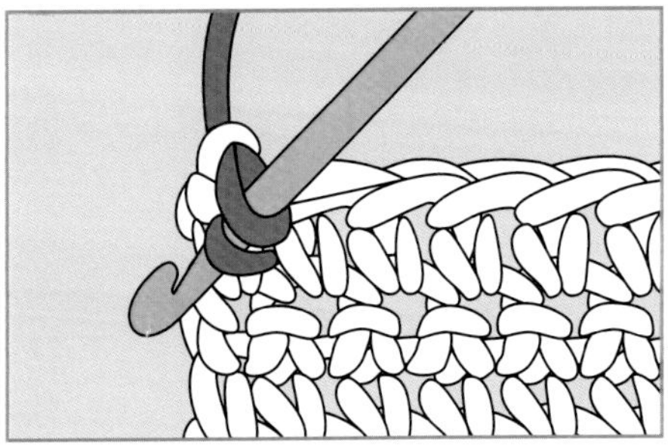

Fig. C

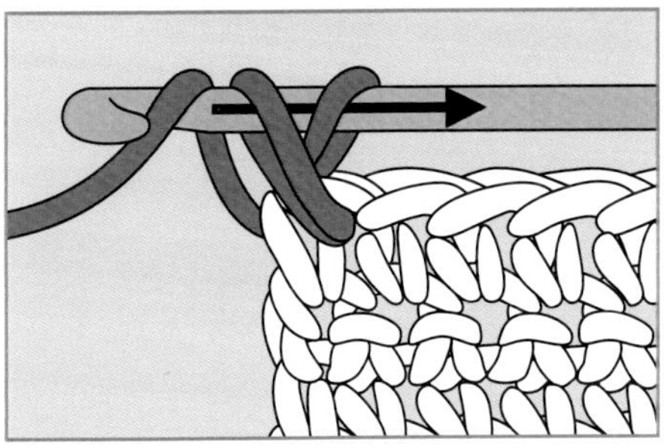

Fig. D

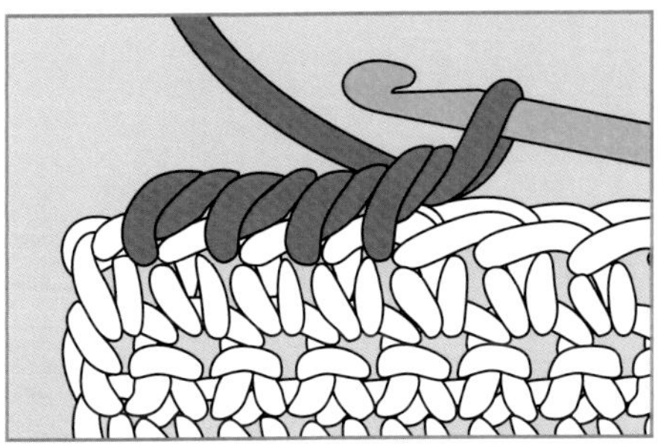

RIGHT STRIP

Work same as Inner Strip through Row 2.

Rows 3 and 4: Work same as Second Side only of Inner Strip.

Join Right Strip to right edge of Inner Strips in same manner.

LEFT STRIP

Work same as Inner Strip through Row 2.

Rows 3 and 4: Work same as First Side only of Inner Strip.

Join Left Strip to left edge of Inner Strips in same manner.

TRIM

Rnd 1:

First Side - With **right** side facing, join Rust with dc in first dc on Right Strip; 3 dc in same st, † skip next dc, dc in sp **before** next dc, ★ 3 dc in next ch-1 sp, skip next 2 dc, dc in sp **before** next dc; repeat from ★ across to last 2 dc, skip next dc, 5 dc in last dc †.

Top Edge - Working across end of rows, skip first row, dc in next row, 3 dc in Leaf, ★ (dc in next row, 3 dc in next row) twice, dc in joining, (3 dc in next row, dc in next row) twice, 3 dc in Leaf; repeat from ★ across to last 2 rows, dc in next row, skip last row.

Second Side - 5 Dc in first dc, repeat from † to † once.

Bottom Edge - Work same as Top Edge, dc in same st as first dc; join with slip st to first dc: 624 dc.

Rnd 2: Ch 3, 3 dc in next dc, dc in next dc, ★ (skip next dc, 3 dc in next dc, skip next dc, dc in next dc) across to center dc of next corner 5-dc group, 3 dc in next dc, dc in next dc; repeat from ★ 2 times **more**, skip next dc, 3 dc in next dc, (skip next dc, dc in next dc, skip next dc, 3 dc in next dc) across to last dc, skip last dc; join with slip st to first dc.

Rnd 3: Ch 1, working from **left** to **right**, work reverse sc in each dc around; join with slip st to first st, finish off.

Design by Sandy Rideout.

INDIAN CORN

●●●○ INTERMEDIATE

Finished Measurement: 49½" x 62¾" (125.5 cm x 159.5 cm)

SHOPPING LIST

Yarn (Bulky Weight) BULKY 5

[3.5 ounces, 127 yards
(100 grams, 116 meters) per skein**]**:

- ☐ Light Grey - 10 skeins
- ☐ Black - 4 skeins
- ☐ Ecru - 2 skeins
- ☐ Gold - 2 skeins

Crochet Hook

- ☐ Size J (6 mm)
  or size needed for gauge

GAUGE INFORMATION

9 dc = 3½" (9 cm),
4 rows = 3¼" (8.25 cm)
One Strip = 9" wide x 62½" long
(22.75 cm x 159 cm)

Gauge Swatch: 3½" wide x 3¼" high
(9 cm x 8.25 cm)
Work same as one Connected Square, page 8: 9 dc.

STRIP (Make 5)

CONNECTED SQUARES

With Light Grey, ch 12.

Row 1: Dc in fifth ch from hook **(4 skipped chs count as first dc)** and in each ch across: 9 dc.

Rows 2-4: Ch 3 **(counts as first dc)**, turn; dc in next 8 dc.

Do **not** finish off; ch 12.

Repeat Rows 1-4 for second Square.

Continue in same manner until 14 Squares are made; finish off.

BORDER

Rnd 1 (Right side)**:** Without turning last Square, join Black with sc in last dc made ***(see Joining With Sc, page 22)***; ch 3, sc in same st, ch 2, working across end of rows, (sc in top of next row, ch 2) 3 times, ★ † working in free loops of beginning ch ***(Fig. 2, page 22)***, (sc, ch 3, sc) in fourth ch, (ch 2, skip next ch, sc in next ch) 3 times, skip last 2 chs and first 2 dc on next Square, (sc in next dc, ch 2, skip next dc) 3 times, (sc, ch 3, sc) in last dc, (ch 2, sc in top of next row) 3 times †, skip first row on next Square, (sc in top of next row, ch 2) 3 times; repeat from ★ 5 times **more**, then repeat from † to † once, ch 2.

Work across second long edge as follows: Working in free loops of beginning ch, (sc, ch 3, sc) in first ch, ch 2, skip next ch, ★ † (sc in next ch, ch 2, skip next ch) 3 times, (sc, ch 3, sc) in next ch, beginning in first row of same Square, (ch 2, sc in top of next row) 3 times, skip last row, (sc in top of next row, ch 2) 3 times on next Square, (sc, ch 3, sc) in first dc, (ch 2, skip next dc, sc in next dc) 3 times †, skip last 2 dc and next 2 chs on next Square; repeat from ★ 5 times **more**, then repeat from † to † once, ch 2; join with slip st to first sc, finish off: 202 ch-2 sps.

Note: Loop a short piece of yarn around any stitch to mark Rnd 1 as **right** side.

Rnd 2: With **right** side facing, join Gold with sc in first ch-3 sp; ch 3, sc in same sp, † ch 2, (sc in next ch-2 sp, ch 2) across to next ch-3 sp, (sc, ch 3, sc) in next ch-3 sp, ★ ch 2, (sc in next ch-2 sp, ch 2) twice, sc in next 2 ch-2 sps, ch 2, (sc in next ch-2 sp, ch 2) twice, (sc, ch 3, sc) in next ch-3 sp; repeat from ★ 12 times **more**, ch 2, (sc in next ch-2 sp, ch 2) across to next ch-3 sp †, (sc, ch 3, sc) in next ch-3 sp, repeat from † to † once; join with slip st to first sc, finish off.

Rnd 3: With Ecru, repeat Rnd 2.

Rnd 4: With Black, repeat Rnd 2.

Rnd 5: With Light Grey, repeat Rnd 2.

LARGE SQUARE

With Light Grey, ch 4; join with slip st to form a ring.

Rnd 1 (Right side)**:** Ch 1, (sc in ring, ch 3) 4 times; join with slip st to first sc: 4 sc and 4 ch-3 sps.

Note: Mark Rnd 1 as **right** side.

Rnd 2: Ch 1, ★ (sc, ch 3, sc) in next ch-3 sp, ch 2; repeat from ★ around; join with slip st to first sc: 8 sc and 8 sps.

Rnd 3: Ch 1, ★ (sc, ch 3, sc) in next ch-3 sp, ch 2, sc in next ch-2 sp, ch 2; repeat from ★ around; join with slip st to first sc: 12 sc and 12 sps.

The method used to connect the pieces is a no-sew joining. Each Square is worked through Rnd 3, then joined to a Strip as Rnd 4 is worked. Holding pieces with **wrong** sides together, work single crochet into spaces as indicated ***(Fig. A)***.

Fig. A

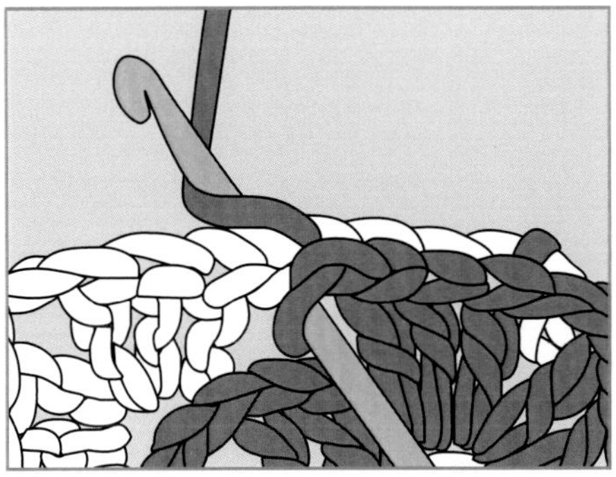

Rnd 4 (Joining rnd)**:** Ch 1, (sc, ch 3, sc) in next ch-3 sp, (ch 2, sc in next sp) 3 times, ch 1, skip 4 ch-2 sps from end ch-3 sp on **Strip** and sc in next ch-2 sp, † ch 1, sc in same ch-3 sp on **Square**, ch 1, sc in next ch-2 sp on **Strip**, ★ ch 1, sc in next sp on **Square**, ch 1, sc in next sp on **Strip**; repeat from ★ 2 times **more** †, holding next Strip with **right** side facing, sc in corresponding ch-3 sp; repeat from † to † once, ch 1, sc in same ch-3 sp on **Square**, ch 2, (sc in next ch-2 sp, ch 2) twice; join with slip st to first sc, finish off.

SMALL SQUARE

Work same as Large Square through Rnd 2.

Rnd 3 (Joining rnd)**:** Ch 1, sc in next ch-3 sp, ch 1, working in space between 2 Strips, sc in same ch-3 sp previously joined, † ch 1, sc in same ch-3 sp on **Square**, ★ ch 1, sc in next ch-2 sp on **Strip**, ch 1, sc in next sp on **Square**; repeat from ★ once **more**, ch 1 †, sc in next 2 sps on **Strip**, repeat from † to † once, sc in next ch-3 sp on same **Strip** and on next Strip, repeat from † to † once, sc in next 2 sps on **Strip**, repeat from † to † once; join with slip st to first sc, finish off.

Make 12 more Small Squares, then a Large Square to complete joining Strips.

Using Placement Diagram as a guide, join remaining Strips in same manner.

PLACEMENT DIAGRAM

Note: Each Strip has 14 Connected Squares.

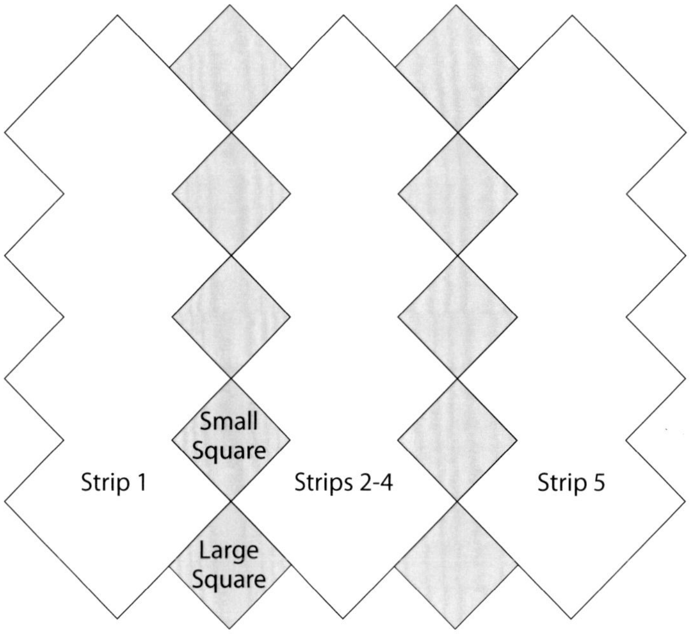

TRIM

With **right** side facing, join Light Grey with sc in any ch-3 sp; ch 3, sc in same sp, (ch 2, sc in next ch-2 sp) around working (sc, ch 3, sc) in each ch-3 sp and working sc in next 2 sps at each "V"; join with slip st to first sc, finish off.

Design by Kathryn Clark.

BOLD STRIPES

●●○○ EASY

Finished Measurement: 49" x 65" (124.5 cm x 165 cm)

SHOPPING LIST

Yarn (Medium Weight) MEDIUM 4

[3.5 ounces, 210 yards (100 grams, 192 meters) per skein]:

- ☐ Grey - 5 skeins
- ☐ Dark Grey - 3 skeins
- ☐ Plum - 3 skeins
- ☐ Cream - 2 skeins
- ☐ Marl - 2 skeins

Crochet Hook

- ☐ Size H (5 mm)

  or size needed for gauge

GAUGE INFORMATION

In pattern,

16 sts and 13 rows = 4" (10 cm)

Gauge Swatch: 4" (10 cm) square

With Dark Grey, ch 17.

Rows 1-13: Work same as Afghan: 16 sc.

AFGHAN

Each row is worked across length of Afghan. When joining yarn and finishing off, always leave a 6" (15 cm) end to be worked into fringe.

With Dark Grey, ch 261.

Row 1 (Right side)**:** Sc in second ch from hook and in each ch across; finish off: 260 sc.

Note: Loop a short piece of yarn around any stitch to mark Row 1 as **right** side.

Row 2: With **right** side facing and working in Back Loops Only ***(Fig. 1, page 22)***, join Cream with sc in first sc ***(see Joining With Sc, page 22)***; sc in each sc across; finish off.

Repeat Row 2 for pattern working in the following stripe sequence: ★ † 1 Row Dark Grey, 9 rows Grey, 1 row Dark Grey, 1 row Cream, 1 row Dark Grey †, 3 rows Plum, 3 rows Marl, 3 rows Plum, 1 row Dark Grey, 1 row Cream; repeat from ★ 5 times **more**, then repeat from † to † once.

FRINGE

Using one 12" (30.5 cm) length of corresponding color, add additional fringe in each row across short edges of Afghan ***(Figs. 6a & b, page 23)***, pulling yarn ends through loop.

Design by Irma Park.

CANYON RIPPLE

●●○○ EASY

Finished Measurement: 36" x 48" (91.5 cm x 122 cm)

SHOPPING LIST

Yarn (Medium Weight) 4

[3.5 ounces, 210 yards
(100 grams, 192 meters) per skein]:

- ☐ Main Color - 5 skeins
- ☐ Color A - 3 skeins
- ☐ Color B - 3 skeins

Crochet Hook

- ☐ Size J (6 mm)

  or size needed for gauge

GAUGE INFORMATION

In pattern,
21 sts = 6" (15.25 cm),
12 rows = 3½" (9 cm)

Gauge Swatch: 6" wide x 3½" high
(15.25 cm x 9 cm)

With Main Color, ch 22.

Rows 1-12: Work same as Body, page 14: 6 sts and 5 ch-4 sps.

STITCH GUIDE

TREBLE CROCHET ***(abbreviated tr)***

YO twice, insert hook in sc indicated, YO and pull up a loop (4 loops on hook), (YO and draw through 2 loops on hook) 3 times.

BODY

Each row is worked across length of Afghan. When joining yarn and finishing off, always leave a 6" (15 cm) end to be worked into fringe.

With Main Color, ch 170.

Row 1 (Right side)**:** Sc in second ch from hook and in each ch across: 169 sc.

Note: Loop a short piece of yarn around any stitch to mark Row 1 as **right** side.

Row 2: Ch 1, turn; sc in first sc, (ch 1, skip next sc, sc in next sc) across: 85 sc and 84 ch-1 sps.

Row 3: Ch 1, turn; sc in first sc, working in **front** of previous row ***(Fig. 4, page 23)*** and in skipped sc in row **below**, dc in skipped sc, (ch 1, dc in skipped sc) across, sc in last sc on previous row: 86 sts and 83 ch-1 sps.

Row 4: Ch 1, turn; sc in first sc, ch 4, ★ skip next ch-1 sp, working **behind** previous row, dc in sc in row **below** next ch-1 sp, ch 4; repeat from ★ across to last ch-1 sp, skip last ch-1 sp and next dc, sc in last sc; finish off: 43 sts and 42 ch-4 sps.

Row 5: With **right** side facing, join Color A with sc in first sc ***(see Joining With Sc, page 22)***, ★ working in **front** of next ch-4, dc in next dc in row **below**, tr in next sc 2 rows **below**, dc in next dc in row **below**, sc in next st on previous row; repeat from ★ across: 169 sts.

Row 6: Ch 1, turn; sc in first sc, (ch 1, skip next dc, sc in next st) across: 85 sc and 84 ch-1 sps.

Row 7: Ch 1, turn; sc in first sc, working in **front** of previous row and in skipped dc in row **below**, dc in skipped dc, (ch 1, dc in skipped dc) across, sc in last sc on previous row: 86 sts and 83 ch-1 sps.

Row 8: Ch 1, turn; sc in first sc, ch 4, ★ skip next ch-1 sp, working **behind** previous row, dc in sc in row **below** next ch-1, ch 4; repeat from ★ across to last ch-1 sp, skip last ch-1 sp and next dc, sc in last sc; finish off: 43 sts and 42 ch-4 sps.

Rows 9-120: Repeat Rows 5-8 for pattern, working in the following stripe sequence: 4 Rows **each** of ★ Main Color, Color B, Main Color, Color A; repeat from ★ 6 times **more**.

Row 121: With Main Color, repeat Row 5; do **not** finish off.

TOP TRIM

Row 1: Ch 1, turn; sc in each st across: 169 sc.

Row 2: Ch 1, turn; slip st in first sc, (ch 1, skip next sc, slip st in next sc) across; finish off.

Row 3: With **right** side facing, join Main Color with slip st in first slip st; slip st in next ch-1 sp, (ch 1, slip st in next ch-1 sp) across, slip st in last slip st; finish off.

BOTTOM TRIM

Row 1: With **right** side facing and working in free loops of beginning ch ***(Fig. 2, page 22)***, join Main Color with slip st in first ch; (ch 1, skip next ch, slip st in next ch) across; finish off.

Row 2: Repeat Row 3 of Top Trim.

FRINGE

Holding 6 strands of matching color together, each 12" (30.5 cm) long, add fringe to center of each stripe across short edge without yarn ends ***(Figs. 6a & b, page 23)***.
Holding 5 strands of matching color together, add fringe in same manner across remaining short edge, pulling both yarn ends of same color through loop.

Design by Anne Halliday.

GOLD STRIKE

●●○○ EASY

Finished Measurement: 48" x 61" (122 cm x 155 cm)

SHOPPING LIST

Yarn (Medium Weight) MEDIUM 4

[3.5 ounces, 205 yards
(100 grams, 187 meters) per skein]:

- ☐ Gold - 7 skeins
- ☐ Brown - 4 skeins
- ☐ Rust - 3 skeins

Crochet Hook

- ☐ Size J (6 mm)
  or size needed for gauge

Additional Supplies

- ☐ Yarn needle

GAUGE INFORMATION

In Center pattern,
16 sc and 16 rows = 4½" (11.5 cm)
One Strip = 9" (22.75 cm) wide

Gauge Swatch: 4½" (11.5 cm) square
Work same as Strip Center, page 17,
through Row 16: 10 sc and 3 ch-2 sps.

STRIP (Make 5)

CENTER

With Gold, ch 17.

Row 1 (Right side)**:** Sc in second ch from hook and in each ch across: 16 sc.

Note: Loop a short piece of yarn around any stitch to mark Row 1 as **right** side and bottom edge.

Row 2: Ch 1, turn; sc in first sc, ch 2, (skip next 2 sc, sc in next 2 sc, ch 2) 3 times, skip next 2 sc, sc in last sc: 8 sc and 4 ch-2 sps.

Row 3: Ch 1, turn; sc in first sc, 2 sc in next ch-2 sp, (sc in next 2 sc, 2 sc in next ch-2 sp) 3 times, sc in last sc: 16 sc.

Row 4: Ch 1, turn; sc in first 3 sc, ch 2, (skip next 2 sc, sc in next 2 sc, ch 2) twice, skip next 2 sc, sc in last 3 sc: 10 sc and 3 ch-2 sps.

Row 5: Ch 1, turn; sc in first 3 sc, 2 sc in next ch-2 sp, (sc in next 2 sc, 2 sc in next ch-2 sp) twice, sc in last 3 sc: 16 sc.

Repeat Rows 2-5 for pattern until Center measures approximately 55½" (141 cm) from beginning ch, ending by working Row 3 or Row 5. Make sure all of the Centers have the same number of rows.

Finish off.

EDGING

Rnd 1: With **right** side facing, join Rust with sc in first sc on last row ***(see Joining With Sc, page 22)***; ch 2, sc in same st and in next 14 sc, (sc, ch 2, sc) in last sc; work 195 sc evenly spaced across end of rows; working in free loops of beginning ch ***(Fig. 2, page 22)***, (sc, ch 2, sc) in first ch, sc in next 14 chs, (sc, ch 2, sc) in next ch; work 195 sc evenly spaced across end of rows; join with slip st to first sc: 426 sc and 4 ch-2 sps.

Rnd 2: Ch 3 **(counts as first dc)**, (dc, ch 2, dc) in next ch-2 sp, ★ dc in each sc across to next corner ch-2 sp, (dc, ch 2, dc) in corner sp; repeat from ★ 2 times **more**, dc in each sc across; join with slip st to first dc: 434 dc and 4 ch-2 sps.

Rnd 3: Ch 1, sc in same st as joining and in next dc, (sc, ch 2, sc) in next ch-2 sp, ★ sc in each dc across to next corner ch-2 sp, (sc, ch 2, sc) in corner ch-2 sp; repeat from ★ 2 times **more**, sc in each dc across; join with slip st to first sc, finish off: 442 sc and 4 ch-2 sps.

Rnd 4: With **right** side facing, join Gold with sc in first ch-2 sp; ch 2, sc in same sp, ★ sc in each sc across to next corner ch-2 sp, (sc, ch 2, sc) in corner ch-2 sp; repeat from ★ 2 times **more**, sc in each sc across; join with slip st to first sc, finish off: 450 sc and 4 ch-2 sps.

Rnd 5: With Brown, repeat Rnd 4; do **not** finish off: 458 sc and 4 ch-2 sps.

Rnds 6 and 7: Repeat Rnds 2 and 3: 474 sc and 4 ch-2 sps.

ASSEMBLY

With bottom edges at same end, whipstitch length of Strips together working through inside loops only ***(Fig. 5b, page 23)***, beginning in second ch of first corner ch-2 and ending in first ch of next corner ch-2.

TRIM

With **right** side facing, join Gold with sc in any sc; sc in each sc around working in joinings as needed to keep piece flat and working (sc, ch 2, sc) in each corner ch-2 sp; join with slip st to first sc, finish off.

Design by Eleanor Albano-Miles.

ENDLESS RIVER

Finished Measurement: 48½" x 60½" (123 cm x 153.5 cm)

●●○○ **EASY**

SHOPPING LIST

Yarn (Medium Weight)

[3 ounces, 145 yards
(85 grams, 133 meters) per skein]:

☐ Blue Mist - 11 skeins

[3.5 ounces, 170 yards
(100 grams, 156 meters) per skein]:

☐ Light Grey - 5 skeins

☐ Blue - 3 skeins

Crochet Hook

☐ Size H (5 mm)

or size needed for gauge

Additional Supplies

☐ Yarn needle

GAUGE INFORMATION

In Center pattern,
8 dc and 4 rows = 2½" (6.25 cm)
One Strip = 8" (20.25 cm) wide

Gauge Swatch: 2½" wide x 2¾" high (6.25 cm x 7 cm)
Work same as Strip Center, page 20, through Row 5.

STRIP (Make 6)

CENTER

With Blue Mist, ch 10.

Row 1: Sc in second ch from hook and in each ch across: 9 sc.

Row 2 (Right side)**:** Ch 3 **(counts as first dc, now and throughout)**, turn; ★ skip next sc, (dc, ch 1, dc) in next sc; repeat from ★ 2 times **more**, skip next sc, dc in last sc: 8 dc and 3 ch-1 sps.

Note: Loop a short piece of yarn around any stitch to mark Row 2 as **right** side and bottom edge.

Row 3: Ch 3, turn; (dc, ch 1, dc) in each ch-1 sp across, skip next dc, dc in last dc.

Repeat Row 3 for pattern until Center measures approximately 54½" (138.5 cm) from beginning ch, ending by working a **wrong** side row. Be sure all of the Centers have the same number of rows.

Last Row: Ch 1, turn; sc in first 2 dc, skip next ch-1 sp, sc in next 2 dc and in next ch-1 sp, sc in next 2 dc, skip next ch-1 sp, sc in last 2 dc; finish off: 9 sc.

EDGING

Rnd 1: With **right** side facing, join Light Grey with dc in first sc on last row ***(see Joining With Dc, page 22)***; ch 1, (dc, ch 2, dc, ch 1, dc) in same st, † ★ skip next st, (dc, ch 1, dc) in next st; repeat from ★ 2 times **more**, skip next st, (dc, ch 1, dc, ch 2, dc, ch 1, dc) in last st; skip first sc row, work (dc, ch 1, dc) in end of each row across to last sc row, skip last sc row †; working in free loops of beginning ch ***(Fig. 2, page 22)***, (dc, ch 1, dc, ch 2, dc, ch 1, dc) in ch at base of first sc, repeat from † to † once; join with slip st to first dc, finish off.

Rnd 2: With **right** side facing, join Blue with dc in first corner ch-2 sp; ch 1, dc in same sp, (dc, ch 1, dc) in each ch-1 sp and in each corner ch-2 sp around; join with slip st to first dc, finish off.

Rnd 3: With **right** side facing, join Light Grey with dc in first corner ch-1 sp; ch 1, (dc, ch 2, dc, ch 1, dc) in same sp, (dc, ch 1, dc) in each ch-1 sp around working (dc, ch 1, dc, ch 2, dc, ch 1, dc) in each corner ch-1 sp; join with slip st to first dc, finish off.

Rnd 4: With Blue Mist, repeat Rnd 2; do **not** finish off.

Rnd 5: Ch 1, ★ (2 hdc, ch 2, 2 hdc) in next corner ch-1 sp, skip next dc, hdc in sp **before** next dc ***(Fig. 3, page 22)***, (hdc in next ch-1 sp, skip next dc, hdc in sp **before** next dc) across to next corner ch-1 sp; repeat from ★ around; join with slip st to first hdc, finish off leaving a long end for sewing.

ASSEMBLY

With bottom edges at same end, whipstitch Strips together working through **both** loops on **both** Strips ***(Fig. 5a, page 23)***, beginning in second ch of first corner ch-2 and ending in first ch of next corner ch-2.

TRIM

With **right** side facing, join Blue with hdc in any corner ch-2 sp ***(see Joining With Hdc, page 22)***; hdc in each hdc around working in joinings as needed to keep piece flat and working 3 hdc in each corner ch-2 sp; join with slip st to first hdc, finish off.

Design by Eleanor Albano-Miles.

GENERAL INSTRUCTIONS

ABBREVIATIONS

ch(s)	chain(s)
cm	centimeters
dc	double crochet(s)
hdc	half double crochet(s)
mm	millimeters
Rnd(s)	Round(s)
sc	single crochet(s)
sp(s)	space(s)
st(s)	stitch(es)
tr	treble crochet
YO	yarn over

SYMBOLS & TERMS

★ — work instructions following ★ as many **more** times as indicated in addition to the first time.

† to † — work all instructions from first † to second † **as many** times as specified.

( ) or [ ] — work enclosed instructions **as many** times as specified by the number immediately following **or** work all enclosed instructions in the stitch or space indicated **or** contains explanatory remarks.

colon (:) — the number(s) given after a colon at the end of a row or round denote(s) the number of stitches or spaces you should have on that row or round.

CROCHET TERMINOLOGY		
UNITED STATES		INTERNATIONAL
slip stitch (slip st)	=	single crochet (sc)
single crochet (sc)	=	double crochet (dc)
half double crochet (hdc)	=	half treble crochet (htr)
double crochet (dc)	=	treble crochet (tr)
treble crochet (tr)	=	double treble crochet (dtr)
double treble crochet (dtr)	=	triple treble crochet (ttr)
triple treble crochet (tr tr)	=	quadruple treble crochet (qtr)
skip	=	miss

Yarn Weight Symbol & Names	LACE 0	SUPER FINE 1	FINE 2	LIGHT 3	MEDIUM 4	BULKY 5	SUPER BULKY 6	JUMBO 7
Type of Yarns in Category	Fingering, size 10 crochet thread	Sock, Fingering, Baby	Sport, Baby	DK, Light Worsted	Worsted, Afghan, Aran	Chunky, Craft, Rug	Super Bulky, Roving	Jumbo, Roving
Crochet Gauge* Ranges in Single Crochet to 4" (10 cm)	32-42 sts**	21-32 sts	16-20 sts	12-17 sts	11-14 sts	8-11 sts	6-9 sts	5 sts and fewer
Advised Hook Size Range	Steel*** 6 to 8, Regular hook B-1	B-1 to E-4	E-4 to 7	7 to I-9	I-9 to K-10½	K-10½ to M/N-13	M/N-13 to Q	Q and larger

*GUIDELINES ONLY: The chart above reflects the most commonly used gauges and hook sizes for specific yarn categories.

●○○○ BEGINNER	Projects for first-time crocheters using basic stitches. Minimal shaping.
●●○○ EASY	Projects using yarn with basic stitches, repetitive stitch patterns, simple color changes, and simple shaping and finishing.
●●●○ INTERMEDIATE	Projects using a variety of techniques, such as basic lace patterns or color patterns, mid-level shaping and finishing.
●●●● EXPERIENCED	Projects with intricate stitch patterns, techniques and dimension, such as non-repeating patterns, multi-color techniques, fine threads, small hooks, detailed shaping and refined finishing.

CROCHET HOOKS																	
U.S.	B-1	C-2	D-3	E-4	F-5	G-6	7	H-8	I-9	J-10	K-10½	L-11	M/N-13	N/P-15	P/Q	Q	S
Metric - mm	2.25	2.75	3.25	3.5	3.75	4	4.5	5	5.5	6	6.5	8	9	10	15	16	19

GAUGE

Exact gauge is essential for proper size. Before beginning your project, make the sample swatch given in the individual instructions in the yarn and hook specified. After completing the swatch, measure it, counting your stitches and rows or rounds carefully. If your swatch is larger or smaller than specified, **make another, changing hook size to get the correct gauge**. Keep trying until you find the size hook that will give you the specified gauge.

JOINING WITH SC

When instructed to join with sc, begin with a slip knot on hook. Insert hook in stitch or space indicated, YO and pull up a loop, YO and draw through both loops on hook.

JOINING WITH HDC

When instructed to join with hdc, begin with a slip knot on hook. YO, holding loop on hook, insert hook in stitch or space indicated, YO and pull up a loop, YO and draw through all 3 loops on hook.

JOINING WITH DC

When instructed to join with dc, begin with a slip knot on hook. YO, holding loop on hook, insert hook in stitch or space indicated, YO and pull up a loop (3 loops on hook), (YO and draw through 2 loops on hook) twice.

BACK LOOP ONLY

Work only in loop(s) indicated by arrow ***(Fig. 1)***.

Fig. 1

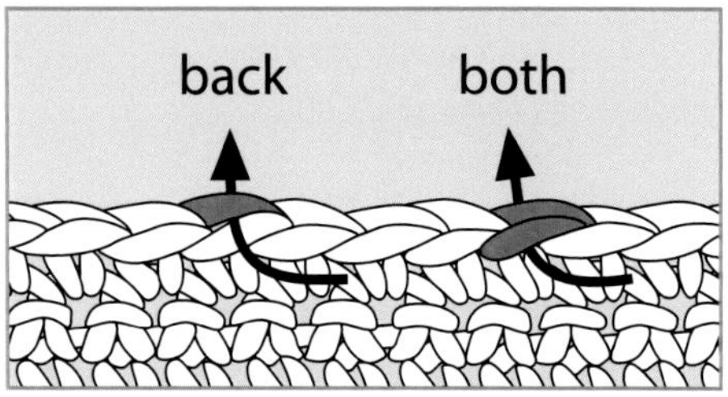

FREE LOOPS OF A CHAIN

When instructed to work in free loops of a chain, work in loop indicated by arrow ***(Fig. 2)***.

Fig. 2

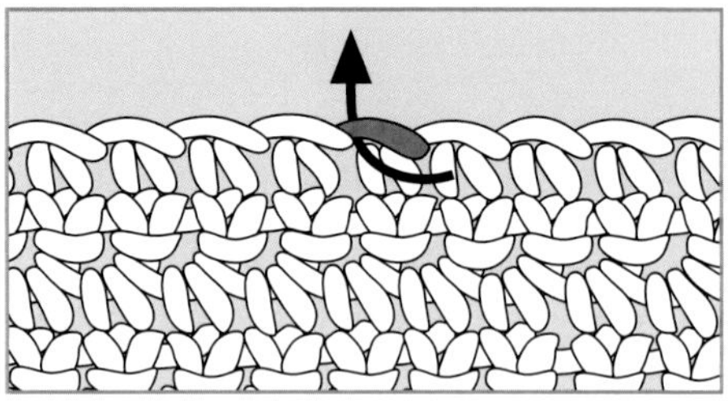

WORKING IN SPACE BEFORE A STITCH

When instructed to work in space **before** a stitch or in spaces **between** stitches, insert hook in space indicated by arrow ***(Fig. 3)***.

Fig. 3

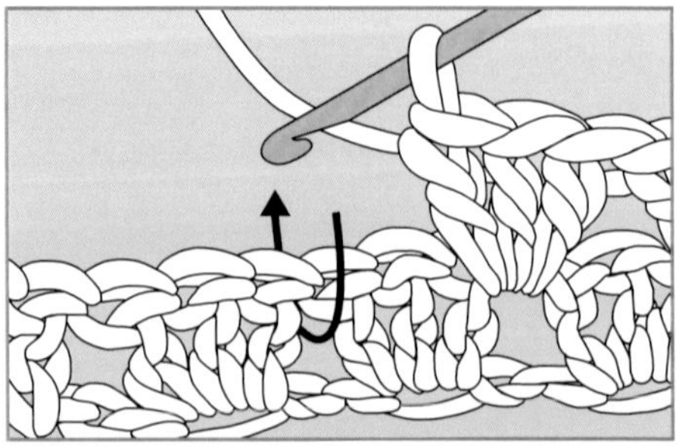

WORKING IN FRONT OF, AROUND, OR BEHIND A STITCH

Work in stitch or space indicated, inserting hook in direction of arrow *(Fig. 4)*.

Fig. 4

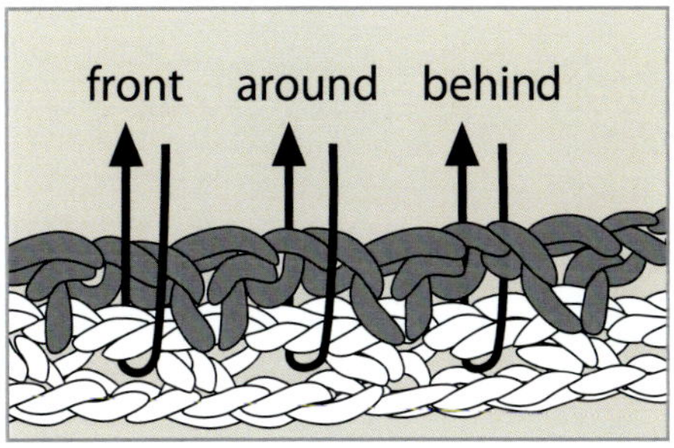

WHIPSTITCH

With **wrong** sides together, sew through both pieces once to secure the beginning of the seam, leaving an ample yarn end to weave in later. Working through **both** loops on **both** pieces *(Fig. 5a)* **or** through **inside** loops only of each stitch on **both** pieces *(Fig. 5b)*, ★ insert the needle from **back** to **front** through the next stitch and pull yarn through; repeat from ★ across. Repeat along the edge, being careful to match stitches.

Fig. 5a

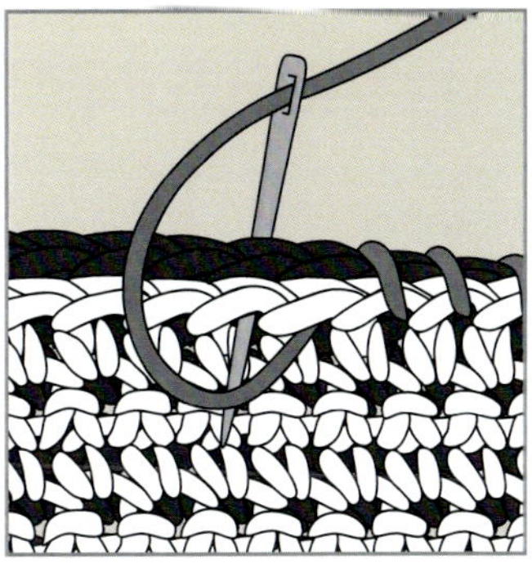

Fig. 5b

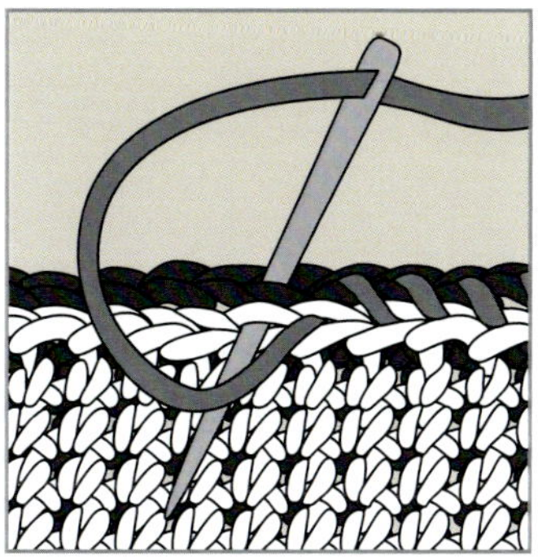

FRINGE

Cut a piece of cardboard 6" (15 cm) square. Wind the yarn loosely and evenly around the cardboard until the card is filled, then cut across one end; repeat as needed.

Hold together as many strands as specified in individual instructions and fold in half.

With **wrong** side facing and using a crochet hook, draw the folded end up through a row and pull the loose ends through the folded end *(Fig. 6a)*; draw the knot up tightly *(Fig. 6b)*. Repeat, spacing as specified in individual instructions.

Lay flat on a hard surface and trim the ends.

Fig.6a

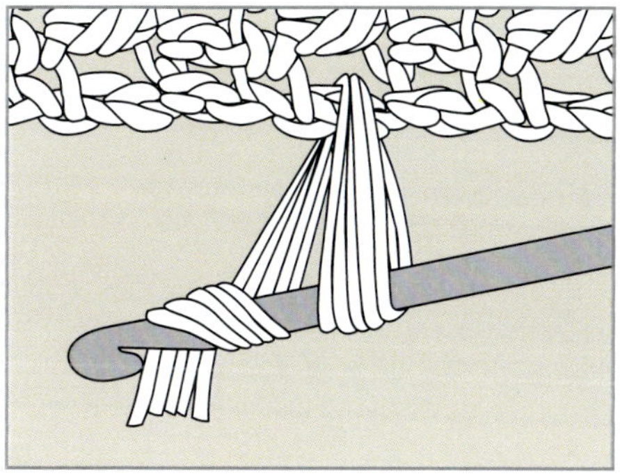

Fig. 6b

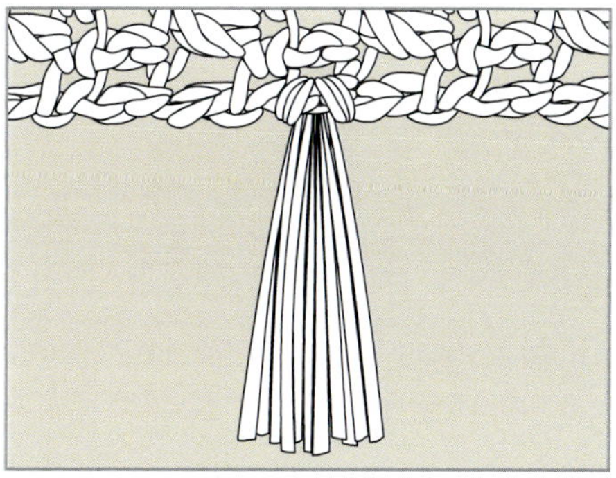

YARN INFORMATION

Each Afghan in this book was made with Medium or Bulky Weight Yarn. Any brand of Medium or Bulky Weight Yarn may be used. It is best to refer to the yardage/meters when determining how many balls or skeins to purchase. Remember, to arrive at the finished size, it is the GAUGE/TENSION that is important, not the brand of yarn.

For your convenience, listed below are the yarns used to create our photography models. Because yarn manufacturers make frequent changes in their product lines, you may sometimes find it necessary to use a substitute yarn or to search for the discontinued product at alternate suppliers (locally or online).

AUTUMN

Lion Brand® Heartland®

Rust - #135 Yosemite

Brown - #126 Sequoia

Ecru - #098 Acadia

Green - #171 Cuyahoga Valley

INDIAN CORN

Lion's Pride® Woolspun®

Light Grey - #099 Linen

Black - #153 Black

Ecru - #098 Fisherman

Gold - #130 Honey

BOLD STRIPES

Patons® Classic Wool Worsted™

Grey - #00224 Grey Mix

Dark Grey - #77044 Mercury

Plum - #77307 Plum Heather

Cream - #00201 Winter White

Marl - #77252 Dark Grey Marl

CANYON RIPPLE

Patons® Classic Wool Worsted™

Main Color - #77215 Heath Heather

Color A - #77219 Seafoam

Color B - #77412 Natural Heather

GOLD STRIKE

Patons® Canadiana™

Gold - #10610 Fool's Gold

Brown - #10013 Timber

Rust - #10630 Burnt Orange

ENDLESS RIVER

Lion Brand® Vanna's Choice®

Blue Mist - #300 Denim Mist

Light Grey - #099 Linen

Blue - #109 Colonial Blue

We have made every effort to ensure that these instructions are accurate and complete. We cannot, however, be responsible for human error, typographical mistakes, or variations in individual work.

Afghans made and instructions tested by Janet Akins, Raymelle Greening, Amanda Loggins, Dale Potter, Barbara Schou, and Margaret Taverner.

Production Team: Instructional/Technical Editor - Cathy Hardy; Editorial Writer - Susan Frantz Wiles; Senior Graphic Artist - Lora Puls; Graphic Artist - Leia Morshedi; Photo Stylist - Lori Wenger; and Photographer - Jason Masters.

Made In U.S.A.